FOOTBALL

CONTENTS

What is football? 3
The game 4
The field 6
Duration 8
The players 10
Laws of the game 11
Fouls 12
Referee—the keepers of the game 15
The FIFA World Cup 18
Current Standing of World's Top Football Clubs 20
Football legends 22
FIFA World Cup 2014 28
FIFA World Cups at a glance 29
Some soccer terms 30
Test Your Memory 31
Index 32

What is football?

Football is an outdoor game played between two teams. Each team tries to score a goal against the other by kicking a spherical ball with the foot.

Football is played in almost all the parts of the world. As a result, there are many varieties of football. The most popular one is called **association football**, commonly known as **soccer**. It is also the most popular sport in the world.

Origins

The earliest records of a game resembling football are documented in a Chinese military manual dated second and third century B.C. At that time it was a form of exercise for the Chinese soldiers known as **cuju** which means 'kick ball'.

The first official international football match was played on the 30th of November, 1872, between England and Scotland. It was held in Scotland at West of Scotland Cricket Club's ground.

Astonishing fact

The largest attendance for a football match ever was 199,854 people in a World Cup match between Brazil and Uruguay on July 1950.

FOOTBALL

The game

In this game, the players are not allowed to use their hands or arms in order to score a goal. They may use their feet or their head to move the ball across the field. However, only the goal keeper is allowed to use his hands or his arms to stop the goal or to throw it back into the play.

Who is a goalkeeper?

A goal keeper, also known as 'goalie', is a player who stands in the goal area between the goalposts to prevent the opposing team from scoring a goal. The goalkeeper is the only player who is permitted to touch the ball with his hands or arms during the play while remaining inside the penalty area. Each team is required to have a goalkeeper on the field at all times during a match.

Astonishing fact

For the first time in FIFA World Cup 2014, the World Cup Final matches will be played using goal-line technology.

The game

In soccer, the goal is scored by kicking the ball into the opposing team's goalposts. Goalposts are a rectangular framework of bars, standing upright on the ground. They are usually covered by a net to catch the ball. The team with maximum number of goals at the end of the full time wins. The goal posts stand 2.44 m high and 7.32 m wide.

The ball

The ball used in the game is a spherical air-filled ball with a circumference of 27 to 28 inches. It weighs around 410-450 grams. The first official soccer ball was designed and built by Charles Goodyear in 1855. It was made from vulcanized rubber.

Now, footballs are made from synthetic leather patches sewn together. A ball based on this design is called the **Buckminster ball** after its inventor, the American architect Richard Buckminster Fuller.

The first Buckminster ball to be used in a world cup was Telstar. It was used in the FIFA World Cup of 1970 held in Mexico.

> **Astonishing fact**
>
> Did you know that a bolt of lightning had killed an entire soccer team during a game in 1998!

FOOTBALL

The field

Football is played on a rectangular piece of land covered with grass or artificial turf with two goal posts in the middle of the either extremes. It is 105 m long and 68 m wide.

The field is marked by various lines drawn on the field. The longer boundary lines are called touchlines. The shorter boundary lines on which the goal posts are placed are called goal lines.

A half-way line connecting the touchlines divides the field into two equal halves. On the middle of the half-way line is located the centre circle. It has a radius of 9.15 metres. The centre of this circle is called the 'centre spot'.

The goal area is marked by two lines which extends 5.5 metres from the inside of each goalpost at right angles to the goal line. These lines are joined by a line drawn parallel to the goal line.

Penalty area is a rectangular box around the goal which extends 16.5 m to each side of the goal and 16.5 m in front of it.

A penalty mark (or a penalty spot) is at 11 m from the goal line. It is located at the midpoint of the goal posts. This spot is used for penalty kicks.

A penalty arc, also called 'the D', adjoins the penalty area, and encloses the area within 9.15 m from the penalty spot.

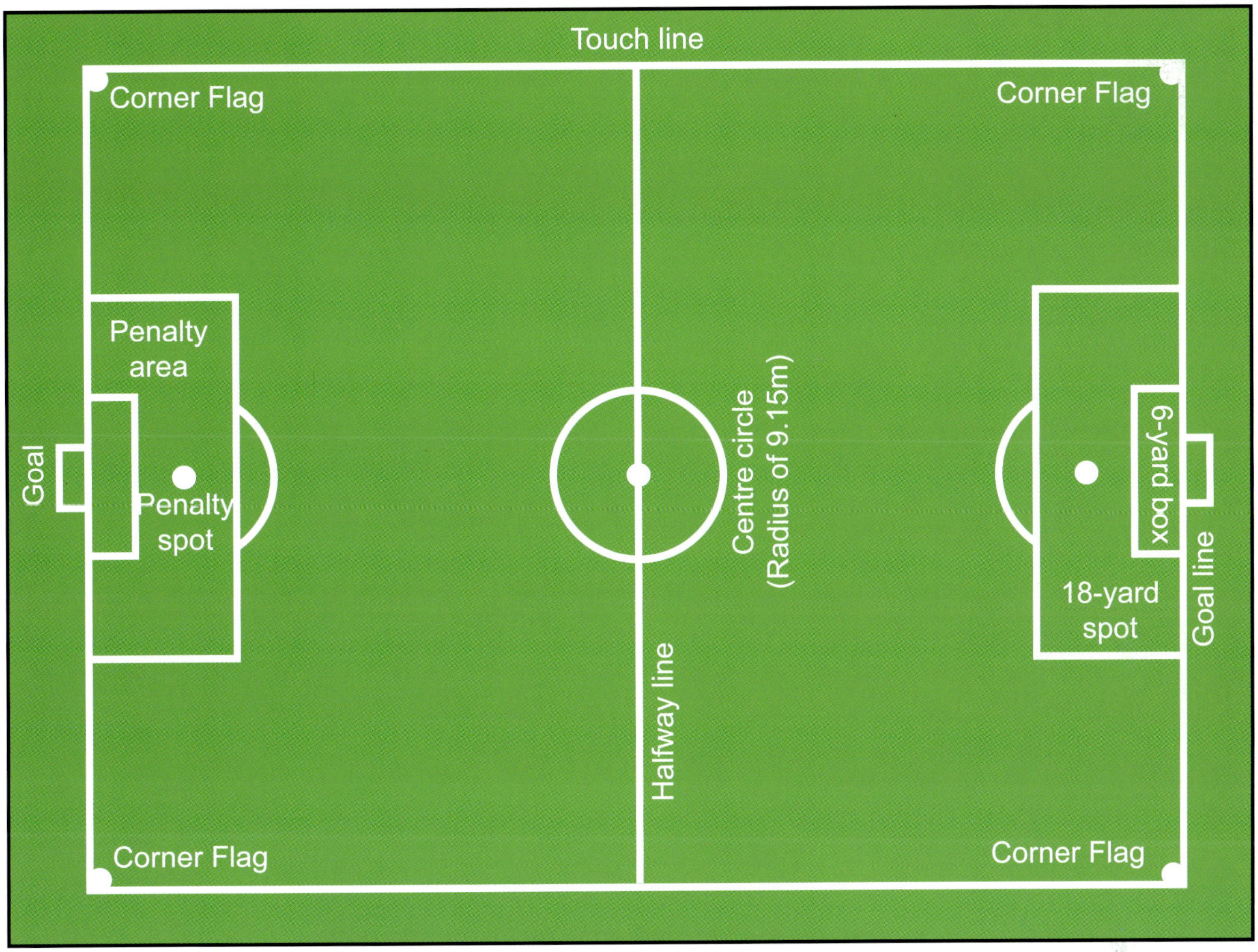

The field

Penalty arc does not form part of the penalty area.

Flagposts of length 1.5 m are placed at the four corners of the field and quarter circles with a radius of 1 m are drawn around them inside the field.

Duration

The game is divided into two periods of 45 minutes each. There is a half-time break of 15 minutes between the two periods. The end of the time is known as full time. The clock is not stopped during the time when the ball is out of play.

An allowance is made for the time lost through substitutions, injured players requiring attention, or other stoppages. This added time is known as stoppage time or injury time. Only the referee can signal the end of the match. The players and spectators are informed of this time by a person holding up a board showing this number.

If the game is tied at the end of full time, it may go into extra time, which consists of two further 15-minute periods. Goals scored during extra time periods count toward the final score of the game.

What is 'ball in, ball out of play?'

There are two basic states of play during the game. From the beginning of each playing period until its end, the ball is in play at all times. When either the ball leaves the field of play, or play is stopped by the referee, the ball becomes out of play. Once the ball goes out of play, the play is restarted the following restart methods depending upon how it went out of play:

A **kick off** is used after a goal or to begin each period of play.

Throw-in is used when the ball has wholly crossed the touchline. It is awarded to the team opposing to the one which last touched the ball.

A **goal kick** is awarded to the defending team when the ball has completely crossed the goal line without a goal having been scored.

A **corner kick** is similar to the goal kick but it is awarded to the attacking team when the ball has last been touched by a player of the defending team.

When the referee has stopped play for any other reason, such as a serious injury to a player, obstruction by an external party, or by a ball becoming defective it is called dropped ball.

FOOTBALL

The players

There are two teams involved in a match of football. The number of players in each team is 11 including the goal keeper. In addition to these, each team is allowed 3 substitute players. There must be at least 7 players present on the field at all times during the play. The match will not start if a team is unable to maintain this minimum number.

The players wear the jersey, shorts, socks and shoes of their respective teams. The goalkeeper, however, must be clearly distinguishable from the rest of the team players. The goal keeper can wear gloves to save himself from finger injuries.

The players must wear shin guards so as to protect them from any serious injury. They are not allowed to wear any jewellery or watches which might cause an injury to the other player.

Laws of the game

The Laws of the game are the rules that help define association football. These laws are published by the sport's highest governing body **FIFA (International Federation of Association Football)**, with the approval of the **International Football Association Board (IFAB)**, the body that writes and maintains the laws. The rules mention the number of players, the length of the game, the size of the field and the ball, etc. The Laws were first drawn up by **Ebenezer Cobb Morley** and approved at a meeting of the Football Association (England) on December 8, 1863. At present, there are 17 laws of the game related to the pitch, the uniforms, number of players, referees, methods of playing and other rules.

Fouls

A foul occurs when something which is considered as wrong according to the rules of the game is done by a player. A foul can be punished by the referee in various ways according to the nature of the foul. These fouls and their respective penalties have been listed in FIFA's Laws of the game.

Direct free kick

If a player commits the following offences, the opposing team is awarded a direct free kick.

- Kicks or attempts to kick an opponent
- Trips or attempts to trip an opponent

- Jumps at an opponent
- Charges an opponent
- Strikes or attempts to strike an opponent
- Pushes an opponent
- Tackles an opponent
- Holds an opponent
- Spits at an opponent
- Handles the ball deliberately (except for the goalkeeper within his own penalty area)

Penalty kick

If any of the above ten offences occur inside the fouling player's own penalty area, the opposing team is awarded a penalty kick.

Indirect free kick

If a goalkeeper commits any of the following four offences inside his own penalty area, the opposing team can be awarded with a direct free kick.

- Controls the ball for more than six seconds with his hands before releasing it
- Touches the ball again after he has released it and before it has came in contact with another player
- Touches the ball with his hands or arms after it has been kicked to him by a team-mate on purpose
- Touches the ball with his hands after he receives it directly from a throw-in taken by a team-mate

An indirect free kick can also be awarded to the opposing team if, according to the referee, a player:

- Plays dangerously
- Obstructs the movement of an opponent
- Stops the goalkeeper from releasing the ball
- Commits an action for which play is stopped, to caution or send off a player

Astonishing fact

During a game of football, a football player can run more than 6 miles!

FOOTBALL

Red card and yellow card

Different from a foul, which happens when players fail to follow the rules of the game, misconduct is related to behaviour of the players towards each other and other officials on the field. If a player misbehaves with the referee or with any other players on the field, like disobeying the referee, or abusing fellow players, or any other sort of unsporting behaviour which dishonours the good spirit of the game, the referee then may penalise him for this. This is done by showing a yellow or a red card to the player. The yellow card is used by the referee to indicate that a player has been warned. This can happen when a player shows unsporting behaviour, dissent through words or actions, disobeys laws of the game, delays the restart of the play, enters or re-enters the playing ground without referee's permission or deliberately leaves the field.

The red card is used to indicate that a player has been sent off. The referee shows this card when a player indulges in severe foul play, violent conduct, spits at an opponent, obstructs the opposing team from scoring a goal by purposely handling the ball, uses abusive language or gestures, is shown a second yellow card. A player who has been shown red card must not only leave the field but also should not come anywhere near it. A player who has been given a yellow card is said to have been 'booked' since the referee writes the player's name in his official notebook.

Coloured cards were first introduced at the 1970 FIFA World Cup.

The official logo of FIFA World Cup 2014 is called 'Inspiration'. Its design is based around a photograph of three victorious hands together raising the World Cup trophy. Its yellow and green colours represent Brazil welcoming the world to their country.

Football goalkeepers did not have to wear different colour shirts until 1909.

14

Referee—the keepers of the game

A **referee** is a person officially appointed by the authorities to watch over the game and ensure proper play. The referee is responsible for maintaining order and enforcing the rules of the game. Referee's decisions regarding the facts of the play cannot be challenged. A player must not disobey a referee's decision under any circumstances.

The referee is assisted by two assistant referees and in some matches also by a fourth official.

Since the fate of the game rests in the referee's hands, it is crucial to be able to understand what he has seen and what he wants.

What is meant by 'advantage'?

When a referee feels that the fouled team still has an advantage in the situation then he will merely point out both his arms. In such a case he will not blow the whistle.

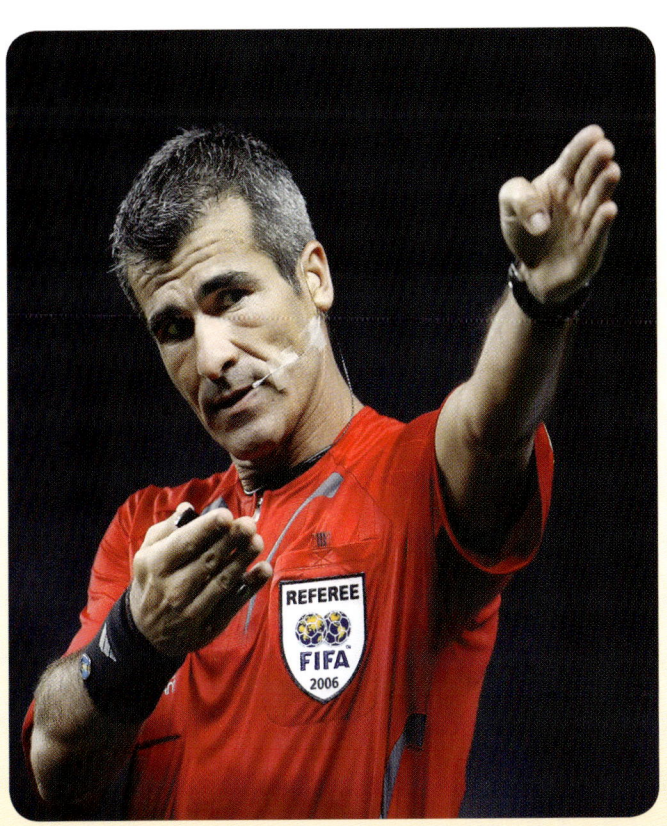

Astonishing fact

In 1966 the World Cup trophy was stolen. It was however found a few days before the tournament by a dog!

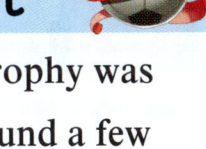

Astonishing fact

A British referee, Ken Aston is the inventor of the concept of using coloured cards. He got the idea when he was sitting in his car at a traffic light!!

FOOTBALL

The whistle

Referees use a whistle to indicate the commencement or restart of play, to stop or delay play due to an infringement or injury, or to indicate that time has expired in the half. The whistle is an important tool for the referee along with verbal, body and eye communication.

AC Milan, famous Italian football club, was actually founded as a cricket team.

A referee blows his whistle when he sees something, usually a foul, or a stoppage in the play, which requires him to immediately stop the play and deal with the situation. The tone of the whistle will often indicate the nature of the foul. A short, quick whistle indicates a lesser foul punishable by a free kick, and longer, harder sound indicate serious fouls punishable by cards or penalty kicks.

Referee—the keepers of the game

Referee signage

Direct free kicks: The referee will blow his whistle and point with a raised arm in the direction of the goal of the team who has been awarded the free kick is attacking.

Indirect free kicks: After signalling for a free kick, if the referee keeps his hand above his head then he is signalling for an indirect free kick. The referee will keep his hand up till the time the ball has been kicked and it has come in contact with another player.

Penalty kick: If the referee points directly to the penalty spot, then he is indicating that a player has committed a direct free kick offense within his own penalty area and a penalty kick has been awarded to the opposing team.

Astonishing fact

Didier Drogba, a footballer from Ivory Coast, had helped stop a civil war in his home country after qualifying for the World Cup.

FOOTBALL

The FIFA World Cup

FIFA is the highest governing body for association football. It is primarily responsible for arranging competitions and most of the rules related to international competitions. FIFA has its headquarters in Zurich, Switzerland. It has now 208 member associations.

There are six regional confederations associated with FIFA:

- **Asia:** Asian Football Confederation (AFC)
- **Africa:** Confederation of African Football (CAF)
- **Europe:** Union of European Football Associations (UEFA)
- **North/Central America & Caribbean:** Confederation of North, Central American and Caribbean Association Football (CONCACAF)
- **Oceania:** Oceania Football Confederation (OFC)
- **South America:** Confederación Sudamericana de Fútbol (South American Football Confederation; CONMEBOL)

Innumerable soccer tournaments take place every year around the globe. Some tournaments take place after a particular period of few years. The biggest international soccer event that takes place once every four years is the FIFA world

> The Fédération Internationale de Football Association (FIFA) was founded in Paris on May 21, 1904.

The FIFA world cup

cup. The last world cup was held in the year 2014 in Brazil. Germany won the 2014 World Cup. It was the 20th world cup. The next FIFA world cup will take place in the year 2018 in Russia.

The FIFA world cup was started in the year 1930 on 13th July. Since then it has taken place once every four years except in the years 1942 and 1946 because of the Second World War.

> The official mascot of the FIFA World Cup 2014 was tatu-bola, an armadillo.

> Adidas' Brazuca was the official ball of the FIFA World Cup 2014.

Current standing of world's top football teams

Ranking	Flag	Country
1	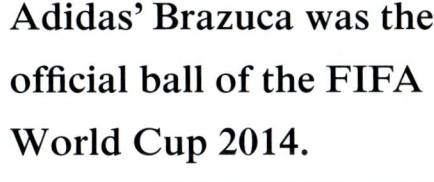	Argentina
2		Germany
3		Belgium
4		Portugal
5		Columbia
6		Spain
7		Brazil
8		Wales
9		Chile
10		England
11		Austria
12		Switzerland

FOOTBALL

Current standing of world's top

Football teams/club logo	Football teams/club
	Barcelona
	Bayern München
	Real Madrid
	Paris Saint Germain
	Juventus
	Atlélico Madrid
	FC Porto
	Manchester City
	Benfica
	Arsenal
	Manchester United
	Sevilla

Famous football teams and clubs

football clubs

Ranking	Country	Based in	Founded in
1	Spain	Barcelona	1899
2	Germany	München	1900
3	Spain	Madrid	1902
4	France	Paris	1970
5	Italy	Torino	1897
6	Spain	Madrid	1903
7	Portugal	Porto	1893
8	England	Manchester	1880
9	Portugal	Lisbon	1904
10	England	London	1886
11	England	Manchester	1902
12	Spain	Seville	1890

FOOTBALL

Football legends

The game has produced some of the most talented sportsmen in the history of humankind. They have taken the game to new levels of excellence increasing its popularity all over the world. Some of the most famous soccer players of all times are:

Name:	Pele (Edson Arrantes de Nascimento)
Born:	23rd October, 1940
Playing position:	Attacking midfielder/Forward
Played for:	Santos, New York Cosmos
National team:	Brazil (1957-1971)
Currently playing for:	Retired
Major achievements:	He is the highest goal scorer in soccer history, with 1281 goals in 1363 matches. He is the only player in the world to have won 3 world cups.

As a kid, since Pele had no money to buy a real ball, he used a stuffed sock instead!!

Pele has scored over 1000 goals in his playing career, the most by any player in the history of the game!!

Name:	Diego Maradona
Born:	30th October, 1960
National team	Argentina
Played for:	Argentinos Juniors, Boca Juniors, FC Barcelona Sevilla, Newell's Old Boys.
Position:	Attacking Midfielder/Second Striker
Currently playing for:	Retired
Major achievements:	He has played in four FIFA World Cup tournaments. In the 1986 World Cup Maradona captained Argentina and led them to their victory over West Germany in the final. He also won the Golden Ball award as the tournament's best player.

Football legends

Maradona was dominantly left-footed. He would often use his left foot even when the ball was more suited for a right foot position!!

Maradona's second goal against England in the 1986 World Cup quarter final was later voted by FIFA as the greatest goal in the history of the World Cup, also called 'the goal of the century'.

Hand of God

In the 1986, world cup quarter final match, the same match in which he scored the goal of the century, just four minutes before that goal, Maradona scored a goal that was fated to remain in controversy forever. He scored the goal with the outside of his fist which the referee failed to see. The goal was therefore considered legitimate. Later he made a statement that the goal was scored, "A little with the head of Maradona and a little with the hand of God."

Name:	Cristiano Ronaldo
Born:	5th February, 1985
National team	Portugal
Played for:	Sporting CP, Manchester United and Real Madrid.
Position:	Forward winger
Currently playing for:	Real Madrid
Major achievements:	Ronaldo currently holds the distinction of being the most expensive player in football history after being transferred from Manchester United to Real Madrid

His second name, 'Ronaldo', was chosen after the then-U.S. president Ronald Reagan, who was his father's favourite actor!!

23

FOOTBALL

Name:	Ronaldo
Born:	22nd September, 1976
National team:	Brazil
Played for:	Cruzeiro, PSV, Barcelona F.C., Internazionale, Real Madrid, Milan and Corinthians
Position:	Striker
Currently playing for:	Corinthians
Major achievements:	He won the European Footballer of the Year in 1997 and again won the award in 2002. He is one of the only two men to have won the FIFA Player of the Year award three times, along with French footballer Zinedine Zidane. He also figures in the FIFA 100, a list of the greatest footballers made by fellow countryman Pelé.

Name:	Zinedine Zidane
Born:	23rd June, 1972
National team:	France
Played for:	Cannes, Bordeaux, Juventus and Real Madrid
Position:	Attacking midfielder
Currently playing for:	Retired
Major achievements:	He was the captain for the team of France for the 2006 World Cup Final where he won the Golden Ball as the tournament's most outstanding player. Zidane also won the Ballon d'Or in 1998.

Zidane and Ronaldo are the only three-time FIFA World Player of the Year winner.

Football legends

Name:	Jari Litmanen
Born:	20th February, 1971
National team:	Finland
Played for:	Reipas, HJK, MyPa and Lahti, Ajax, FC Barcelona, Liverpool, Hansa Rostock, Malmö and Fulham
Position:	Attacking midfielder, second striker
Currently playing for:	Lahti of the Finnish Premier Division and Finland's national football team (Captain)
Major achievements:	He is considered to be Finland's greatest player ever. He was selected as the Best Finnish player of the last 50 years by the Football Association of Finland in November 2003.

Name:	Enzo Francescoli
Born:	12th November, 1961
National team:	Uruguay
Played for:	River Plate, Wanderers, Racing Club, Paris Olympique Marseille, Cagliari and Torino
Position:	Attacking midfielder
Currently playing for:	Retired
Major achievements:	He has played 72 times for his national team between 1982 and 1997, making him the player with the maximum number match appearances in Uruguayan international football.

FOOTBALL

Name:	Johan Cruyff
Born:	25th April, 1947
National team:	Netherlands
Played for:	Ajax, Barcelona, Los Angeles Aztecs, Washington Diplomats, Levante and Feyenoord
Position:	Attacking midfielder, Second striker
Currently playing for:	Retired
Major achievements:	He has won the Ballon d'Or award three times, in 1971, 1973 and 1974. He is widely regarded as one of the greatest players of all time.

Name:	Lionel Messi
Born:	24th June, 1987
National team:	Argentina
Played for:	F.C. Barcelona
Position:	Forward/Winger
Currently playing for:	F.C. Barcelona
Major achievements:	Messi had received several Ballon d'Or and FIFA World Player of the Year nominations by the age of 21. He won both by the age of 22!!

Football legends

Name:	David Beckham
Born:	2nd May, 1975
National team:	England
Played for:	AC Milan, Los Angeles Galaxy, Major League Soccer, Manchester United, and Real Madrid
Position:	Midfielder
Currently playing for:	Los Angeles Galaxy
Major achievements:	During his time under the Manchester United, the club won the Premier League title six times, the FA Cup title twice and the UEFA Champions League in 1999.

Beckham joined the youth squad of Manchester United in July of 1991, at the tender age of sixteen!!

Name:	Ronaldinho
Born:	21st march 1980
National team:	Brazil
Played for:	Gremio, Paris Saint-Germain, Barcelona, AC Milan
Position:	Winger/ Attacking mid-fielder
Currently playing for:	AC Milan
Major achievements:	Ronaldhino was awarded the FIFA Confederations Cup Golden Ball and Golden Shoe in the year 1999. He has also won the FIFA World Player of the year award twice in the years 2004 and 2005. He has been listed in FIFA 100, the list of century's greatest footballers made be Pele. Also he was a part of the FIFA World Cup All Star Team in 2002.

FOOTBALL

FIFA WORLD CUP 2018

This time the grandest stage of all-FIFA World Cup 2018-is set in Russia for football lovers across the globe. An eagerly anticipated event, the FIFA World Cup 2018 will take place from June 14 - July 15, 2018. This is the first time that the World Cup is taking place in the former Soviet Union and the first time in Europe since 2006.

A total of 32 countries from across the globe have qualified to play in this tournament. These countries have been divided into 8 groups and will be competing against each other in a total of 64 matches. A total number of 12 venues have been set for these matches.

Do you know during the world cup in Russia, the participants and fans would be able to come to Russia without needing the Visa just before and during the competition!

FIFA World Cups at a glance

Year	Hosted by	Won by	Runner-up
1930	Uruguay	Uruguay	Argentina
1934	Italy	Italy	Czechoslovakia
1938	France	Italy	Hungary
1950	Brazil	Uruguay	Brazil
1954	Switzerland	West Germany	Hungary
1958	Sweden	Brazil	Sweden
1962	Chile	Brazil	Czechoslovakia
1966	England	England	West Germany
1970	Mexico	Brazil	Italy
1974	West Germany	West Germany	Netherlands
1978	Argentina	Argentina	Netherlands
1982	Spain	Italy	West Germany
1986	Mexico	Argentina	West Germany
1990	Italy	West Germany	Argentina
1994	United States	Brazil	Italy
1998	France	France	Brazil
2002	Korea Republic & Japan	Brazil	Germany
2006	Germany	Italy	France
2010	South Africa	Spain	Netherlands

Some soccer terms

Dribbling: In association football, dribbling refers to the moving of a ball around a player through short skilful kicks or touches with the legs. Dribble is one of the toughest skills to learn.

Equaliser: An equaliser is a type of goal scored by a team that ties the game or equals the score.

Forwards: Forwards also known as attackers and strikers, are the players in a team in association football who play nearest to the opposing team's goal. Usually there are two forwards in a football team.

Ghost goal: Ghost goal is a term used to describe an uncertain goal in which it is hard to decide whether the ball crossed the goal line or not.

Defender: A defender is a player whose role is to prevent the opposition from attacking. There are four types of defender: centre back, sweeper, full back and wing back.

Cap: A cap is a match appearance in sports for a team, such as a school, county or an international team. The origin of the term lies in the practice of awarding an item of headgear, usually cap, in the United Kingdom to every player participating in an international match of association football.

Own goal: An own goal is a goal scored by a player by accident against his or her own team.

Penalty shootout: A penalty shootout is a method sometimes used in a tied soccer game to decide which team moves to the next level of a tournament or wins the tournament.

Rainbow kick: The rainbow kick is a trick kick in which a player steps over the ball and makes it move forward over their head in an arc while running forward with the ball, and rolling the ball up the back of his leg with the other foot.

Stramash: A stramash occurs when there are several players in the 6-yard box, trying to score a goal or/and trying to save a goal. It appears to be very messy and is one of the most entertaining aspects of the game.

Test Your MEMORY

1. When was the first official international soccer match held and where?
2. Who designed the first vulcanized rubber ball and when?
3. What was the name of the first Buckminster ball and when was it first used?
4. What is the standard duration of a soccer game (excluding the half-time break)?
5. What are the standard dimensions of a soccer field?
6. What is the minimum number of players that should be present on the field at all times during the game?
7. What kind of a kick is awarded by the referee when a player strikes another player?
8. In which FIFA World Cup were the red and yellow cards first introduced?
9. What does FIFA stand for?
10. Where are the headquarters of FIFA currently located?
11. When did the first FIFA World Cup take place?
12. When and where will the next FIFA World Cup take place?

Index

A
Association football 3

B
ball 3, 4, 5, 8, 9, 11, 12, 13, 14, 17, 22, 23
Buckminster ball 5

C
Cap 30

D
Defender 30
direct free kick 12, 13, 17
Dribbling 30

E
Equaliser 30

F
FIFA 5, 11, 12, 14, 18, 19, 22, 23, 24, 26, 27, 28, 29
FIFA World Cup 5, 14, 22, 27, 28
Football 3, 6, 11, 18, 20, 22, 23, 25, 27
Forwards 30
full time 5, 8

G
Ghost goal 30
goal 3, 4, 5, 6, 7, 9, 10, 14, 17, 22, 23, 28
goal area 4, 6
goal keeper 4, 10, 28
goal lines 6

I
Indirect free kick 13

O
Own goal 30

P
penalty area 4, 7, 12, 13, 17
penalty kick 12, 17
penalty mark (or penalty spot 7
Penalty shootout 30

R
Rainbow kick 30
red card 14

S
Soccer 3, 26
Stramash 30

T
touchlines 6

Y
yellow card 14